THE HONEYBEES

THE HONEYBEES

with illustrations by Colette Portal

and text by Franklin Russell

Alfred A. Knopf ❧ New York

Library of Congress Catalog Card Number: AC 67-10599
This is a Borzoi Book, published by Alfred A. Knopf, Inc.
© Copyright, 1967, by Franklin Russell
Illustrations © Copyright, 1967, by Colette Portal
All rights reserved under International and Pan-American Copyright
Conventions. Distributed by Random House, Inc. Published
simultaneously in Toronto, Canada, by Random House of Canada Limited.
Manufactured in the United States of America

It is early spring.
The sun shines with cold light.

Pale shadows darken the grass
And the hive of bees stirs, sleepy and warm.

At first the bees move cautiously
from the hive
Testing the warmth of the outside air.

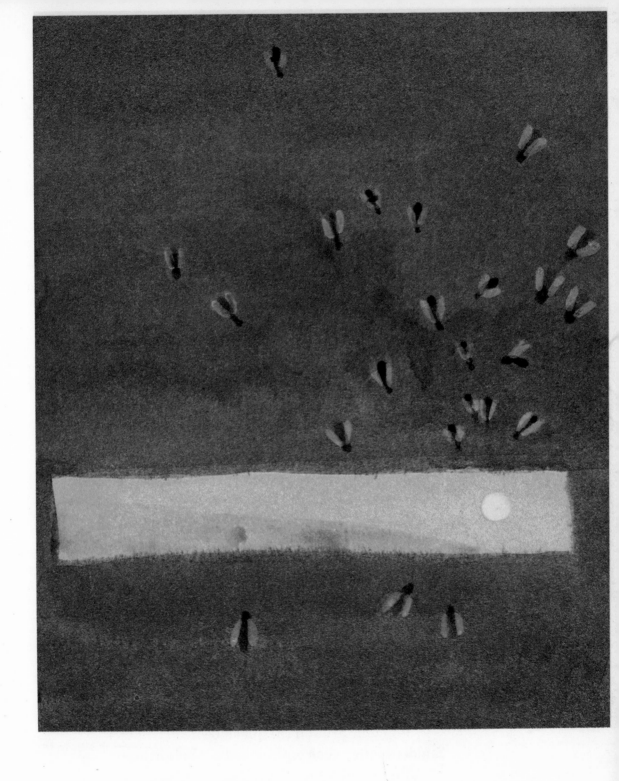

When the land glows green and the first flowers of spring appear
The bees know it will soon be time to move, time
to seek out the new season.

One morning half the bees in the hive gather
    together around the queen bee.
Suddenly they rush out toward the bright sun,
    their queen with them.

A murmur, a buzz, a groan of wings in the wind:
A swarm of thousands of bees is in search of a
    new home.

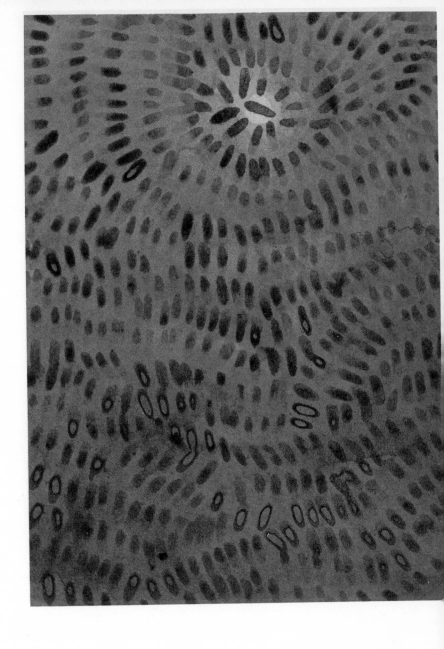

When the queen rests on a branch
The bees cluster around her in a dark hot bundle
While scout bees seek out
    a place for a new hive.

Soon the place is found and the bees move to
    their tasks
And their new home begins to take shape.

Thin strips of wax grow on their bellies.
They chew it, and with it they build a city
    of cells.

The workers know what to build: large cells
 for the future queens, smaller cells for
 drones, or males.
They build the smallest cells for the thousands
 of workers yet to be born.
They build rows of cells to store the
 food of the hive: bee-bread and honey.

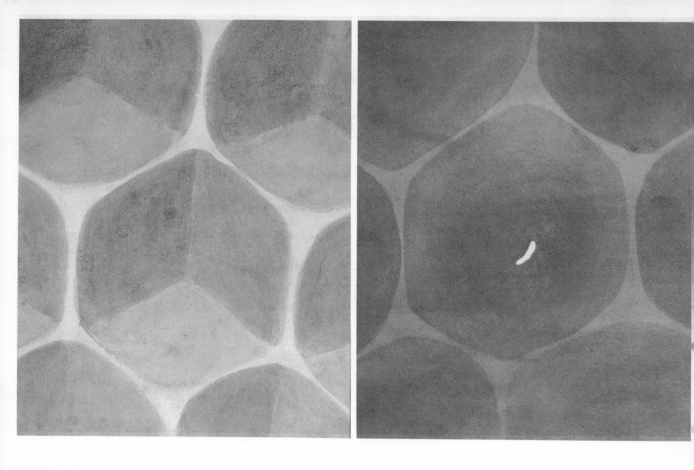

Each cell has six walls that fit neatly against
    the ones around it
And as fast as they are built the bees fill them.

While the workers gather nectar and pollen
    the queen begins her work.
She drops one egg in each cell, lays two eggs a minute
    night and day without rest.

Then the first egg hatches and a white grub wriggles.
Workers hatch in thousands and drones in hundreds.

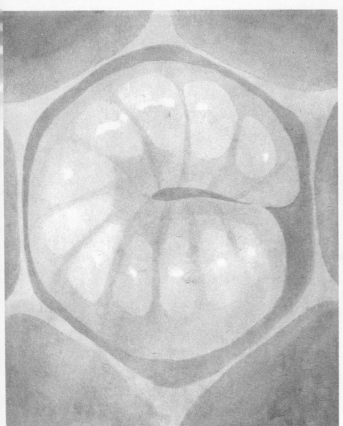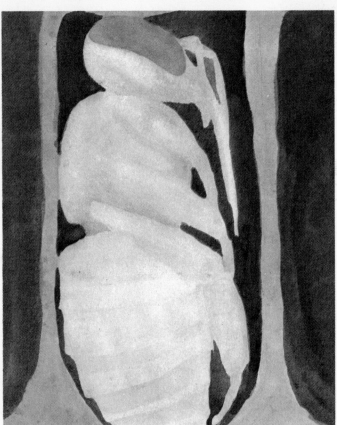

The bees work on and on, filling the cells with honey
While the grubs grow many, many times larger
    and press against the walls of their tiny prisons.

They will be workers and drones.
Some of them, a very few, are being fed a
    special royal jelly
And this food will turn them, almost magically,
    into the queens of the future.

A new worker bee bites through the cell cover and is born.
Her wings dry, her body darkens quickly.
Her eyes, made of ten thousand surfaces,
    glow in the soft light of early summer.
They await the sight of flowers not yet seen.

She will join her sisters and work at first
    in the buzzing hive.
She will help feed the young bees in the cells
    or clean the hive
    or fan the air with her wings.
She will move through jostling masses of bees
    intent on their many tasks.

Until one day she is ready to leave the hive
And join in the dance of the flowers.

The flowers of summer are rich
Forming jungles of color where worker bees
        hunt all day.

They jostle and push, thrust and lunge
among the flowers.

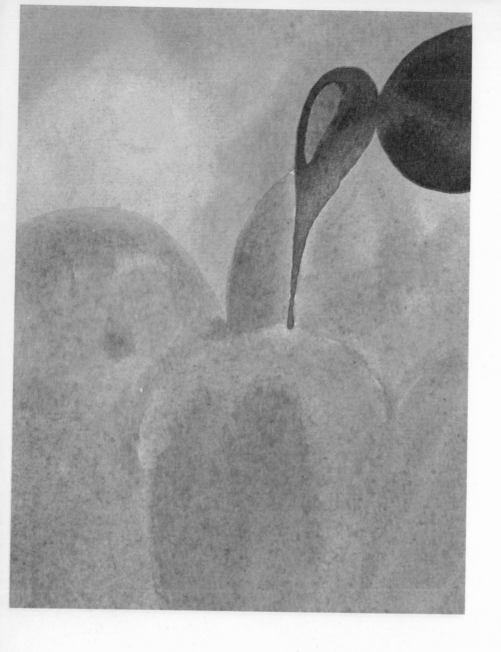

Across the petals, the bees hasten
In endless search for food.

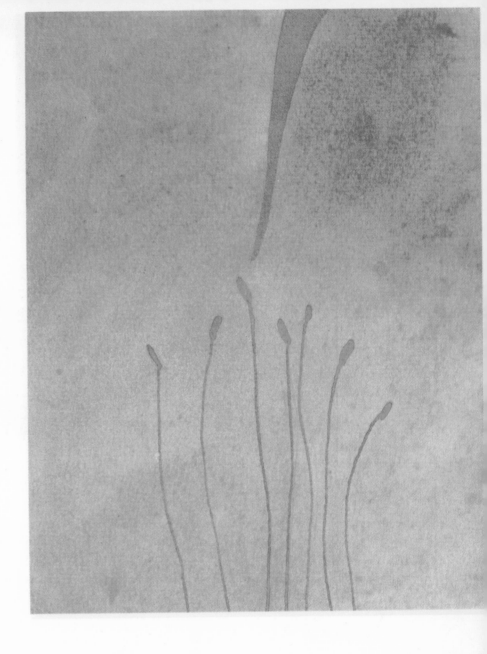

They reach out of sight deep into pastel halls
    where the light of the sky is dim
To suck the sweet drops of nectar which they
    will transform into honey.
Pollen, the yellow dust of flowers that will
    become their bread, clings to their legs.

Then, their wings frayed with flying,
    burdened with nectar and pollen
    they flit to the hive
As the warming sun watches their work.

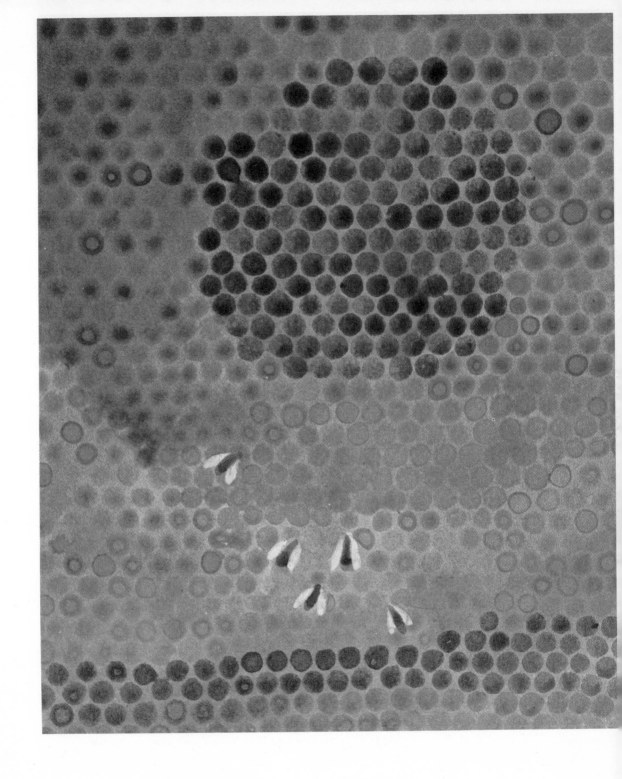

In the hive, a golden flood of honey pours in
from the glistening land
And row upon row of cells overflow with food.

Heat grows and the queen works frantically
    at laying her eggs
Surrounded by her watchful attendants.

Cooling air is fanned by her workers
To preserve food and new bees growing in cells.

One day, as thousands of new bees are born,
    the hive is too crowded
But the old queen knows what to do.
She gathers half the bees of the hive around her
And in one joyful swarm leads them into the open
    in search of a new home.

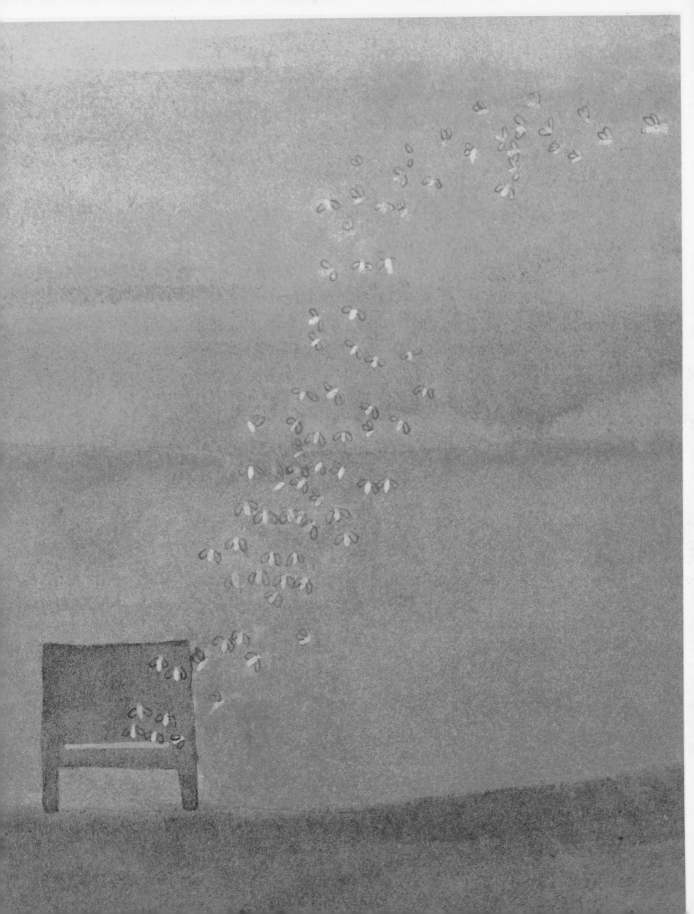

In the old hive, a princess hatches and a
new order begins.

Watched by attendants, she moves along the
cells of her sister princesses
And kills them before they can be born.
Only one queen can reign over the hive.

Then on a bright clear day, the young queen
rises high in the sky with one strong drone.
Close to the sun, warmed by it, they mate:
A new generation of bees begins in her body.

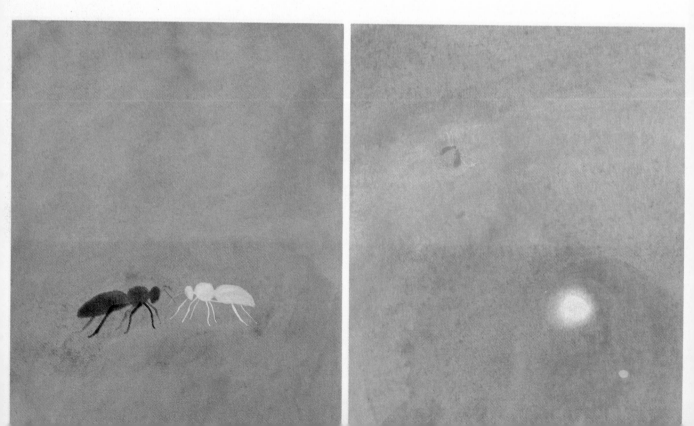

The mating done, they tumble from the sky.
The drone dies and the young queen hurries
    back to the hive.

She begins to lay her eggs immediately.

The heat of summer fills the air and the
drones drowse away their final days.
They do not gather honey nor do they work.
And the busy hive now has no use for them.

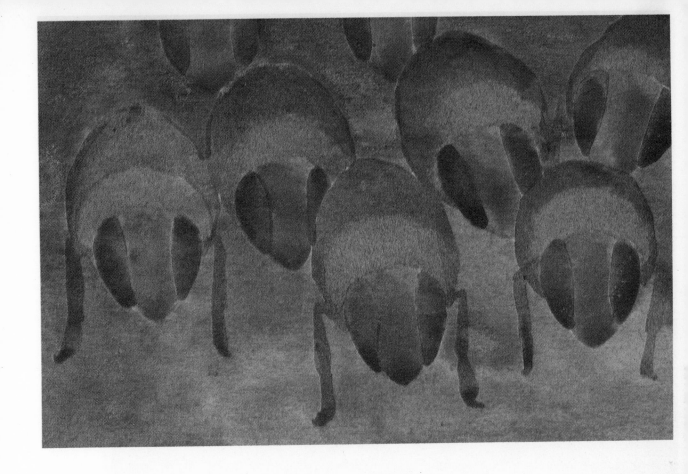

One day the worker bees advance on the drones,
    silent and menacing.
The drones are slain or driven off to die in trees.

Summer is fading. Life slows. The cells of
    the hive are stocked for winter.
Late blooms hide among the grasses.

Red autumn lurks in the leaves
As a few worker bees still fly around in search
of the last flowers.

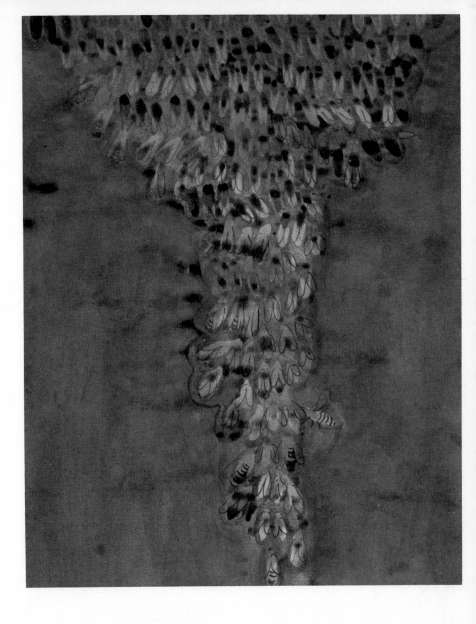

Cold days come. The bees cling together for
        warmth.
Their queen is among them, cared for and
        protected.
Within her body are the eggs of workers, drones,
        and future queens, all to be born next spring.

Then it will be her turn to take half the hive
        away to a new home.

The year's work is done
And the bees welcome the long waiting time.

The sun sinks to a winter's death.
The earth shrivels and dries.

A murmur of air runs down corridors of honey
And the hive of the bees is asleep.

Text set in Century Expanded
Composed at Rapid Typographers, Inc., New York City
Printed by Rae Publishing Co., Cedar Grove, New Jersey
Bound by Economy Bookbinding Corp., Kearny, New Jersey
Typography by Robert Giusti